TWO EYES
A NOSE
and A MOUTH

For my dad,
Seymour Grobel,
whose words and ideas were the inspiration for this book.

To my family, friends, and Brooklyn neighbors,
whose enthusiastic support and participation helped to make
this book a reality; and to Renée, Bernette, Edie, and Sonia,
who helped bring it together . . . thank you all.

Written, photographed, and designed by Roberta Grobel Intrater.

Library of Congress Cataloging-in-Publication Data

Intrater, Roberta Grobel.
Two eyes, a nose, and a mouth / by Roberta Grobel Intrater.
p.   cm.
"Cartwheel Books."
ISBN 0-590-48247-5
1. Physical anthropology—Juvenile literature. 2. Human anatomy—Variation—Juvenile literature.
3. Body, Human—Social aspects—Juvenile literature. I. Title.
GN62.8.I57   1995
573—dc20   94-18390
                                                              CIP

12 11 10 9 8 7 6 5 4 3   7 8 9/9 0/0
Printed in Singapore

First Scholastic printing, April 1995

TWO EYES
·A NOSE·
and A MOUTH

BY ROBERTA GROBEL INTRATER

Cartwheel
·B·O·O·K·S·®

SCHOLASTIC INC.
New York   Toronto   London   Auckland   Sydney

Two eyes, a nose, and a mouth,

they're the first things that we see

on millions and millions of faces,

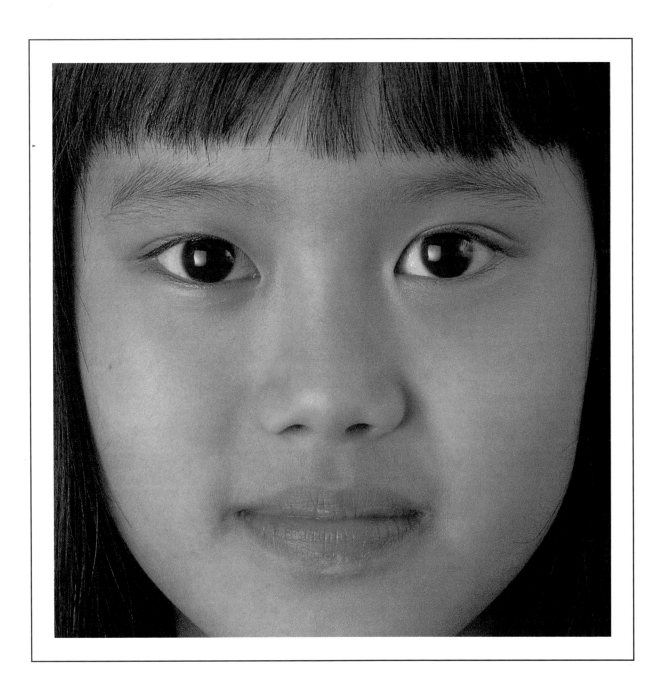

from Tibet to Tennessee.

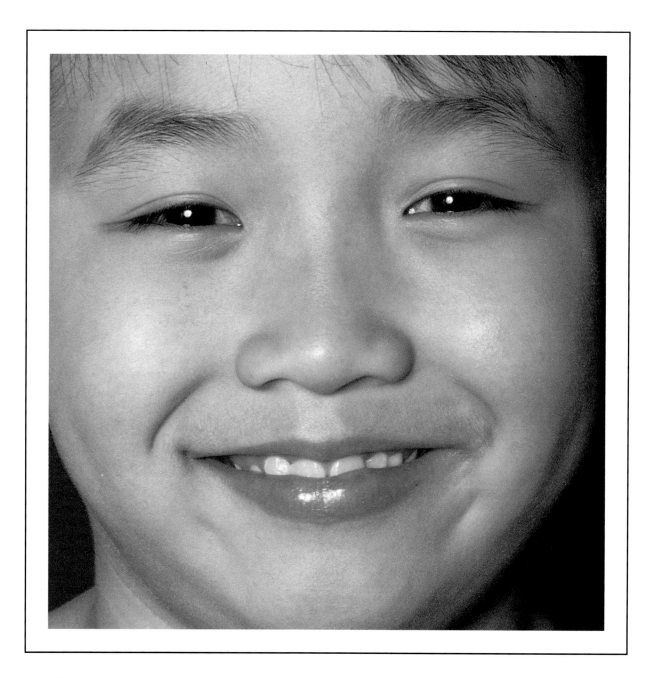

Some eyes are shaped like almonds;

others are big and round.

And what about the eyebrows?

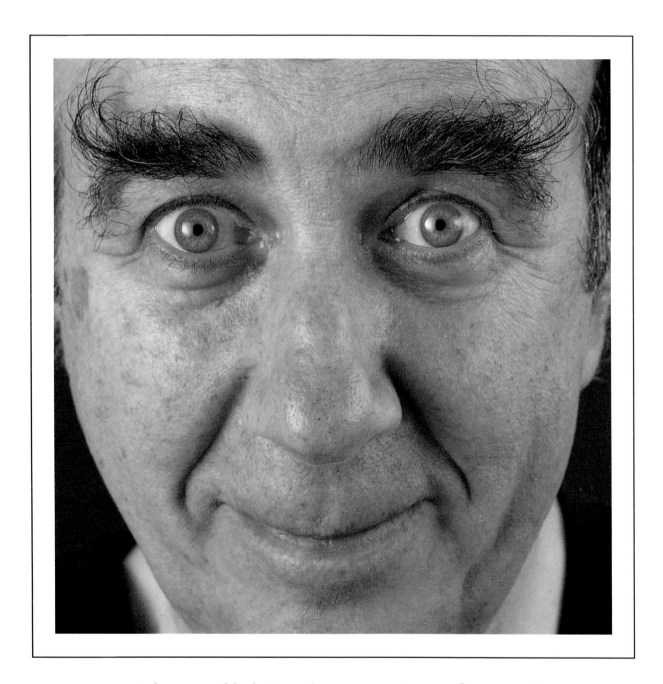

Why, all kinds can be found.

Noses can be short and wide,

or turn out long and bumpy.

Some are small and curve up . . .

and some are kind of lumpy.

When it comes to mouths, it's plain to see

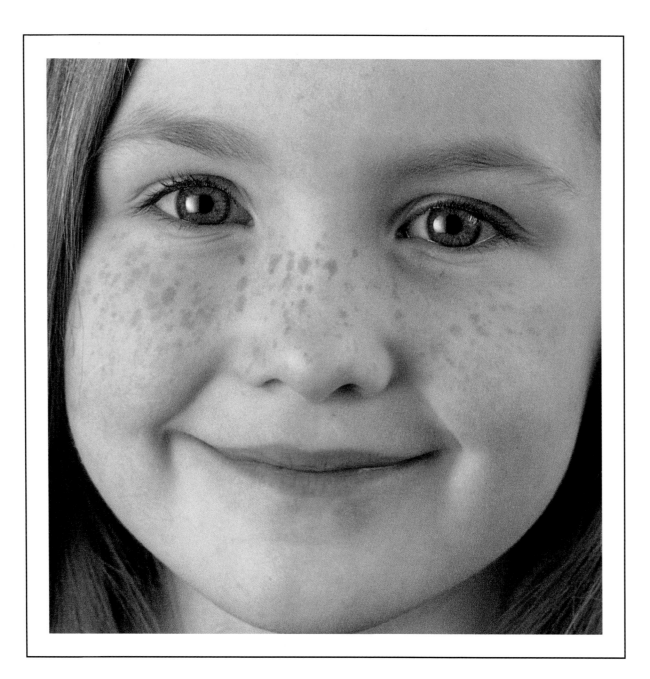

the variety is just fine.

Some have lips that are full and broad

while others are thin as a line.

Isn't it amazing

how changing a feature or two

makes millions and millions of faces,

yet no one looks just like you.

Imagine how dull the world would be

if everyone looked like you or me.

Over and over we'd see the same face

till we'd wish for another to take its place.

How lucky we are

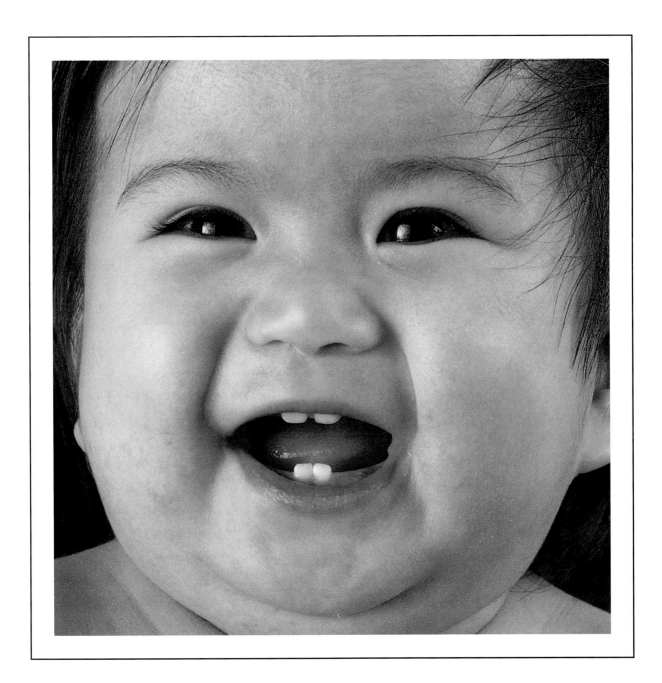

the world isn't that way.

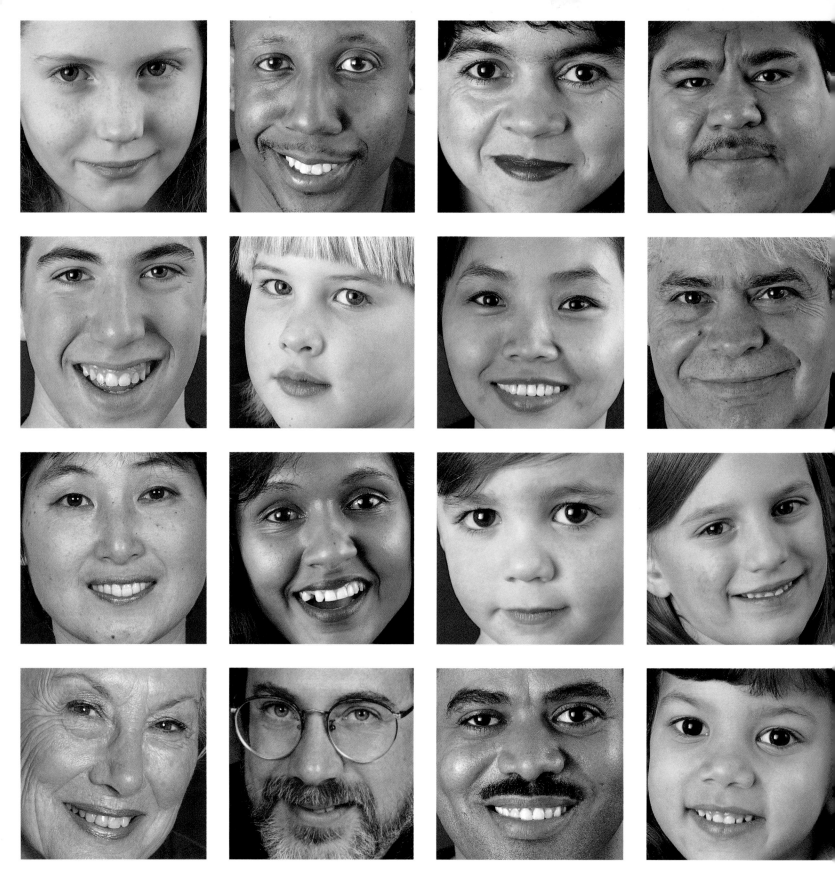

Our differences make us special,

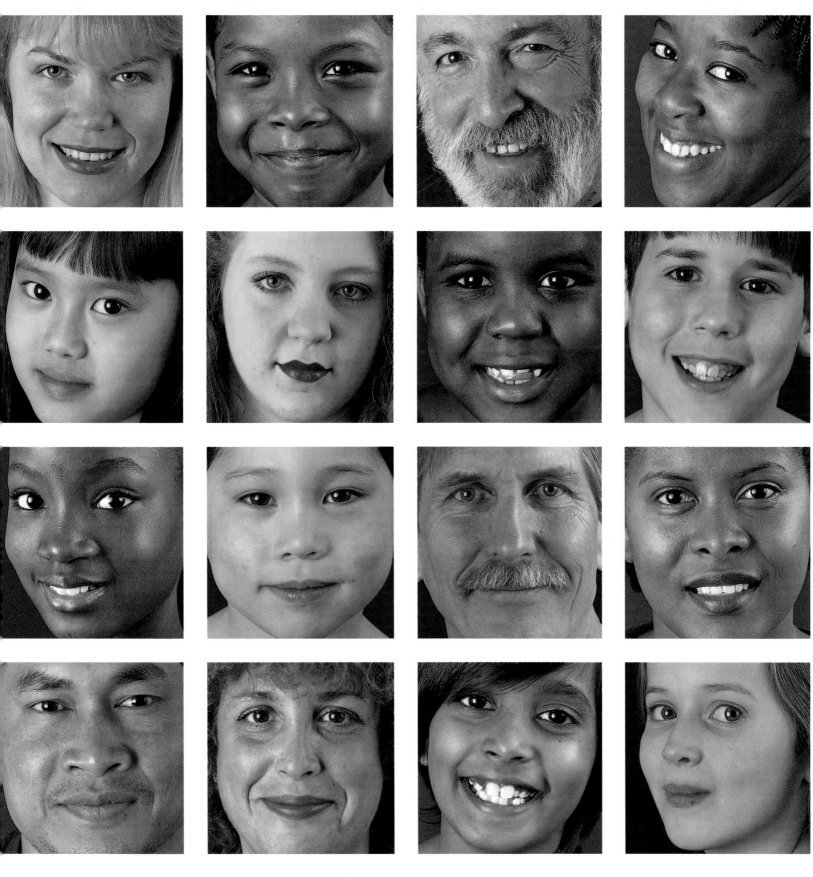

wouldn't you say?

Paste
your
picture
here.